An Apple Pie I Will NOT Buy

Based on a true story

Written by Noreen C. Phillips

Illustrated by Katie Howard

Archway Publishing books may be ordered through booksellers or by contacting:

Archway Publishing
1663 Liberty Drive
Bloomington, IN 47403
www.archwaypublishing.com
844-669-3957

Because of the dynamic nature of the Internet, any web addresses or links contained in this book may have changed since publication and may no longer be valid. The views expressed in this work are solely those of the author and do not necessarily reflect the views of the publisher, and the publisher hereby disclaims any responsibility for them.

Any people depicted in stock imagery provided by Getty Images are models, and such images are being used for illustrative purposes only.
Certain stock imagery © Getty Images.

Interior Image Credit: Katie Howard

ISBN: 978-1-6657-0098-6 (sc)
ISBN: 978-1-6657-0099-3 (hc)
ISBN: 978-1-6657-0097-9 (e)

Print information available on the last page.

Archway Publishing rev. date: 04/07/2021

Acknowledgements:

Photo of Nana's Pie Plate: Martha Swenson
Editing/suggestions: Michelle, Andy, Marlys, Fran,
Mia, Saul, Amber, Matt, Christine, Anya, Emily,
Lila, Wendy, Ella, Nash, Meers Scale Co., Adyn,
Cecelia, Georgie, Maggie, Katie B., Emma, Elizabeth,
Mary, Genevieve, Patrick, Beth, ClareRita, Isaac,
AgnesAnne and everyone who encouraged me.
Thanks

Dedicated to Michelle Klima Phillips,
whose illness revealed our dependence
on one another to be a truth both
inescapable and profoundly moving

&

To Andy and Michelle's grandsons
Fio and Wendell
[whose mother knows a good book
title when she hears one]

It was a wintry day in December.

My friend asked,
"Need or want
anything from town?"

"Need or want?" I asked with a
frown. Is there a difference?

"Very much so: A need you **must** have, like food or a home, but wants are just trimmings, like candy or chrome," he said.

I replied: Then I need
nothing, but a tasty
apple pie, please buy!

Much to my surprise, he fairly shouted, "I will NOT buy an apple pie. An apple pie I will NOT buy!"

Is it because it is a treat and not a need? I meekly asked.

"No! Treats are just fine if you keep them in line," he snapped.

I asked: Well then, why?

"Why what?" he asked, as if he didn't know.

I, ever so patiently answered, **WHY
won't you buy me an apple pie?**

Said he quite loudly: "WHY?"

More loudly still: "WHY?"

Now a shrill: "WHY?"

Why? I countered in a soft lilt.

And as if it made sense, he announced:

"Because, my friend, there are some
rules one does NOT bend. I will buy
you a banana cream pie, a key lime
pie, a cherry pie, a raisin pie, a custard
pie, why **even** a chicken pot
pie, but an apple pie I will **NOT** buy!"

No apple pie,

I sighed.

Said he, "Don't be ridiculous! Apples I
WILL BUY to make a tasty pie."

NEVER FAIL PIE CRUST

2 cups flour	¾ cup lard
1 teaspoon salt	

work with fork until crumbly, add:

¼ c. water	1 tablespoon vinegar
1 egg [optional]	

Blend all ingredients together; knead slightly. Divide into
4 parts. Makes enough for 2 – two crust pies. Roll out to
fit pie plate.

Never say Never!

Haralson
Prairie Spy

APPLE PIE   400 10 minutes; 350 about 50 minutes
6-7   tart apples
¾ to 1 cup sugar
2 tablespoons all-purpose flour
½ to 1 teaspoon cinnamon
Dash nutmeg & salt
2 tablespoons butter *(or more!)*
Pastry for 2 crust 9-inch pie plate

Pare and slice apples. Combine dry ingredients and
mix with apples. Line 9-inch pie plate with pastry,
fill with apples, dot with butter Cover with pastry.

Isn't that a lot of work? Said I with less of a lilt.

"Nonsense, far easier

than making a quilt."

Off to town...................and back,

apples in hand.

Together we worked, to beat the band.

In no time we had a tasty pie and it was grand, entirely grand.

Yes, well I remember that day in December.

That day with many a twist and turn.
I with ever so much to learn.

"Some rules one DOES NOT bend," with
emphasis said my good friend.

Leave wants on the shelf!
Needs of others tend first,
lest wants become a curse,
and all our bubbles we burst.

We **NEED** one another, so help the other. Remember,
working together makes everything, much, much better!

And,

Oh yes,

do NOT ask my friend

To buy an apple pie, because

[Readers, you've got this. So altogether
let's hear the answer]

an apple pie

he will NOT
buy!

Nana's oft used pie plate was used one more time.

The Story Behind the Story

Love, for Thomas Aquinas, means to consistently will and choose the good of the other. Love, therefore, requires sacrifice because we human beings tend, more often than not, to put ourselves before others. Thomas More refers to "that obstructing thing called 'I.'"

Our narrator and the narrator's good friend are married. Over their forty plus years together they have learned what it means to truly love. As the story begins, the wife has cancer. It is not their first fight with the illness, not even their second. It is their third and last.. Despite their pain and limitations, each one will continue to do all in their power to will and choose the good of the other.

Each and every need or want of the wife is provided [usually in triplicate] until one day in December. The wife requests the purchase of an apple pie. You know the response: "An apple pie I will NOT buy. I will NOT buy an apple pie!" Having lived on an apple orchard, the husband has some set opinions on all things apple. Cider is made on a small antique press and special apples are used to make apple pies. And LIKE LOVE, you don't **buy** an apple pie, you **work** at it!

About the Author

Noreen C. Phillips has taught high school in Fairbanks, Alaska; run a buffing machine in St. Paul, Minnesota; worked at a family apple orchard in Lake Elmo, Minnesota; served as a public defender, working with adults and children, in Ramsey County, Minnesota; and worked at a unique daycare in Maplewood, Minnesota. Her apple pies are legendary in more than one state.

Printed in the United States
by Baker & Taylor Publisher Services